THE GOSPEL OF JOHN:
Jesus' Teachings

*A 4-week course to help
senior highers understand Jesus'
teachings in the Gospel of John*

by David Adams

Group®

The Gospel of John: Jesus' Teachings
Copyright © 1990 Group Publishing, Inc.

Fourth Printing, 1994

Credits
Edited by Stephen Parolini
Cover designed by Jill Bendykowski and DeWain Stoll
Interior designed by Judy Atwood Bienick and Jan Aufdemberge
Illustrations by John Burns
Photo on cover by Brenda Rundback
Photo on p. 17 by Jim Bradshaw
Photo on p. 26 by Richard West
Photo on p. 42 by David Priest

ISBN 1-55945-208-0
Printed in the United States of America.

CONTENTS

New Life

Help teenagers understand what it means to have "new life" in Christ.

We're All Sheep

Help teenagers know what it means to be a part of Jesus' flock.

The Vine We Cling To

Help teenagers learn about a Christian's responsibilities.

Follow Me

Help teenagers understand Jesus' command to "feed my sheep."

THE GOSPEL OF JOHN: JESUS' TEACHINGS

"*S*unday school taught me all *about* Jesus, but how can I get to *know* him better?"

• • •

Christian teenagers know about Jesus. From the time they were old enough to sing "Jesus Loves Me" they've been learning who Jesus is. But do they really know Jesus' teachings? Jesus had a lot to say to the people of his time. But his teachings are more than historical writings—they're important messages for Christians today.

A great place to begin learning about Jesus' teachings is the Gospel of John. This unique Gospel focuses on Jesus' life like no other. Many Christians point to the book of John as the reason for their faith.

Teenagers have many demands on their time, so they don't always make time for spiritual development. By helping them see the importance of Jesus' teachings in the book of John, you'll be helping kids develop their faith—so they can better deal with the other demands on their time.

In this course, you'll help teenagers understand Jesus' teachings and how their faith makes a difference. Kids will begin to understand the importance of a commitment to Jesus.

Not only will this course help teenagers grow, it'll meet kids' needs. The book of John speaks to many of kids' top concerns. Consider the following statistics about Christian teenagers' top concerns.

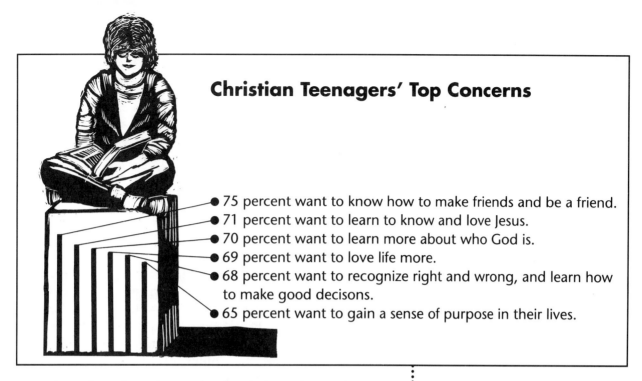

Christian Teenagers' Top Concerns

- 75 percent want to know how to make friends and be a friend.
- 71 percent want to learn to know and love Jesus.
- 70 percent want to learn more about who God is.
- 69 percent want to love life more.
- 68 percent want to recognize right and wrong, and learn how to make good decisons.
- 65 percent want to gain a sense of purpose in their lives.

By reading about how Jesus shepherds his "sheep," kids will discover what it means to know and love Jesus. Your kids will discover how to love life more as they learn what it means to have new life in Christ.

The book of John will help teenagers gain a sense of purpose in life as they discover Jesus' teaching to "feed my sheep." And from Jesus' example, kids will learn how to make good decisions about right and wrong.

Help your kids see how Jesus' messages in the Gospel of John can be relevant to their lives. In this four-week course, your kids will enjoy a Bible study like no other. Through active-learning experiences, kids will feel what Jesus' disciples felt, and learn what they learned. Students will also grow closer to the other class members; their desire for friendship skills will be met as they participate in the class.

The Gospel of John: Jesus' Teachings will bring Jesus' teachings alive for your teenagers.

By the end of this course your students will:
- be able to identify the underlying theme of the Gospel of John;
- read through the Gospel of John;
- understand the concept of a spiritual life;
- examine what it means to be Jesus' followers;
- explore a Christian's responsibilities;
- discover the significance of Jesus' Death and Resurrection; and
- commit to sharing what they've learned with others.

COURSE OBJECTIVES

HOW TO USE THIS COURSE

ACTIVE LEARNING

Think back on an important lesson you've learned in life. Did you learn it from reading about it? from hearing about it? from something you experienced? Chances are, the most important lessons you've learned came from something you experienced. That's what active learning is—learning by doing. And active learning is a key element in Group's Active Bible Curriculum.

Active learning leads students in doing things that help them understand important principles, messages and ideas. It's a discovery process that helps kids internalize what they learn.

Each lesson section in Group's Active Bible Curriculum plays an important part in active learning.

The **Opener** involves kids in the topic in fun and unusual ways.

The **Action and Reflection** includes an experience designed to evoke specific feelings in the students. This section also processes those feelings through "How did you feel?" questions and applies the message to situations kids face.

The **Bible Application** actively connects the topic with the Bible. It helps kids see how the Bible is relevant to the situations they face.

The **Commitment** helps students internalize the Bible's message and commit to make changes in their lives.

The **Closing** funnels the lesson's message into a time of creative reflection and prayer.

When you put all the sections together, you get a lesson that's fun to teach—and kids get messages they'll remember.

BEFORE THE 4-WEEK SESSION

● Read the Introduction, the Course Objectives and This Course at a Glance.

● Decide how you'll publicize the course using the art on the Publicity Page (p. 9). Prepare fliers, newsletter articles and posters as needed.

● Look at the Bonus Ideas (p. 45) and decide which ones you'll use.

● Read the opening statements, Objectives and Bible Basis for the lesson. The Bible Basis shows how specific passages relate to senior highers today.

● Choose which Opener and Closing options to use. Each is appropriate for a different kind of group. The first option is often more active.

● Gather necessary supplies from This Lesson at a Glance.

● Read each section of the lesson. Adjust where necessary for your class size and meeting room.

● The approximate minutes listed give you an idea of how long each activity will take. Each lesson is designed to take 35 to 60 minutes. Shorten or lengthen activities as needed to fit your group.

● If you see you're going to have extra time, do an activity or two from the "If You Still Have Time . . ." box or from the Bonus Ideas (p. 45).

● Dive into the activities with the kids. Don't be a spectator. The lesson will be more successful and rewarding to both you and your students.

HELPFUL HINTS

● The answers given after discussion questions are responses your students *might* give. They aren't the only answers or the "right" answers. If needed, use them to spark discussion. Kids won't always say what you wish they'd say. That's why some of the responses given are negative or controversial. If someone responds negatively, don't be shocked. Accept the person, and use the opportunity to explore other angles of the issue.

THIS COURSE AT A GLANCE

Before you dive into the lessons, familiarize yourself with each lesson aim. Then read the scripture passages.
- Study them as a background to the lessons.
- Use them as a basis for your personal devotions.
- Think about how they relate to teenagers' circumstances today.

LESSON 1: NEW LIFE

Lesson Aim: To help teenagers understand what it means to have "new life" in Christ.

Bible Basis: John 3:1-21.

LESSON 2: WE'RE ALL SHEEP

Lesson Aim: To help teenagers know what it means to be a part of Jesus' flock.

Bible Basis: John 10:1-18 and Psalm 23.

LESSON 3: THE VINE WE CLING TO

Lesson Aim: To help teenagers learn about a Christian's responsibilities.

Bible Basis: Isaiah 5:1-7 and John 15:1-7.

LESSON 4: FOLLOW ME

Lesson Aim: To help teenagers understand Jesus' command to "feed my sheep."

Bible Basis: Mark 16:15-20 and John 21:15-19.

PUBLICITY PAGE

Grab your senior highers' attention! Copy this page, then cut and paste the art of your choice in your church bulletin or newsletter to advertise this course on the Gospel of John. Or copy and use the ready-made flier as a bulletin insert. Permission to photocopy this clip art is granted for local church use.

Splash this art on posters, fliers or even postcards! Just add the vital details: the date and time the course begins, and where you'll meet.

It's that simple.

THE GOSPEL OF JOHN: Jesus' Teachings

Come to _____

On _____

At _____

Discover how to live an exciting life as a Christian!

NEW LIFE

When we become Christians, we're told we begin "new lives" in Christ. But do teenagers really understand what it means to begin new lives as Christians? By listening to Nicodemus' question and Jesus' answer in the Gospel of John, teenagers can gain insight into what it means to have new life in Christ.

To help teenagers understand what it means to have "new life" in Christ.

Students will:
- **examine what it means to have "new life";**
- **compare the differences between old life and new life;**
- **understand the importance of love for Christians; and**
- **discover that God's commitment to them calls for a response.**

Look up the following scripture. Then read the background paragraphs to see how the passage relates to your senior highers.

In **John 3:1-21**, Jesus tells Nicodemus he must be "born again."

Nicodemus, a prominent religious leader in Jerusalem, came to Jesus secretly, since he was afraid of being seen with Jesus. Nicodemus was searching for answers to questions about the meaning of his life. This conversation may've been the turning point of Nicodemus' life.

Teenagers are similar to Nicodemus in that they encounter Jesus—often in secret—with questions of their own. They, like Nicodemus, can begin to learn what "new life in Christ" means for their lives. They can learn how great God's love is for them. And they can learn how a new life in Christ changes attitudes and behaviors.

Section	Minutes	What Students Will Do	Supplies
Opener (Option 1)	5 to 10	**Old and New**—Choose pictures representing old life and new life.	Tape, newsprint, magazines, markers
(Option 2)		**Question and Answer**—Brainstorm important questions and answers.	Paper, pencils
Action and Reflection	10 to 15	**Towers**—Try to build towers out of cards.	3×5 cards, tape
Bible Application	10 to 15	**New Life**—Examine what Jesus says about becoming a Christian.	Bibles, paper, pencils
Commitment	5 to 10	**New-Life Love**—Complete a handout and think about the importance of love for Christians.	"New-Life Love" handouts (p. 17), pencils
Closing (Option 1)	5 to 10	**Love and Relationships**—Tell their greatest hopes for their relationships with each other.	
(Option 2)		**New-Life Resolutions**—Affirm each other's strengths, and resolve to live new lives in Christ.	

The Lesson

OPENER
(5 to 10 minutes)

Note to the Teacher: Encourage your kids to read the book of John during this course. Give a copy of the "Contract and Reading Guide" (p. 16) to students at the beginning or end of today's session. Have kids each read and sign the contract portion—then tear it off and give it to you. Check up on kids' reading progress each week.

OPTION 1: OLD AND NEW

Tape a sheet of newsprint with the heading "New Life" on the wall. Next to it, tape another sheet of newsprint with the heading "Old Life." Form teams of no more than six. Have teams each choose a name. Give teams each a supply of magazines, markers and tape. On "go," have teams search for pictures depicting new life and old life. Have them tear out each picture, write their team name on it and tape it to the appropriate newsprint.

Allow three minutes for teams to compete in this race. After you call time, have kids form a semicircle facing the newsprint.

For each picture, ask the kids if they understand why it's placed there. Discuss any questionable pictures, and discard ones that clearly don't fit. Total the number of pictures from each group and declare the winner.

Ask:

● **How easy was it to decide which pictures depicted old life or new life? Explain.** (Very easy, new life is clearly defined; difficult, some things could've gone either way.)

● **Why is there such a variety of pictures?** (You didn't define "new" or "old"; we didn't know what to look for.)

If weather and time allow, have teenagers go outside and search for evidences of new life. When they return, have them discuss how they feel when they see new life developing. Discuss how this new life in nature is like a new life in Christ.

Say: **In the book of John, Jesus taught about gaining a new life by being "born again." But many people didn't understand what Jesus meant. Today we're going to take a close look at what new life is all about.**

☐ OPTION 2: QUESTION AND ANSWER

Form two groups, and give each group some paper and a pencil. Tell the groups they're going to help answer the great questions of the universe. Tell one group to decide what the 10 most important questions in the universe are. Have them use "what" or "how" questions such as "What's the meaning of life?" and "How can we have world peace?" Tell the other group to decide what the most likely answers are to the 10 most important questions. Tell kids not to eavesdrop but to make up answers to the questions *they'd* ask. Have groups each number their list from 1 to 10.

After a few minutes, form one group. Have the "question" group read the first question and the "answer" group read the first answer. Some combinations will probably be humorous.

After you've covered all the questions and answers, ask:

● **How easy is it to ask or answer these questions, and why?** (It's tough because it's hard to agree on what the questions are or to know what they might be.)

● **Is knowing the answers to these questions really important to you?** (No, we don't think about these things; yes, I'm intrigued by these questions.)

● **Where can we get the real answers to many of these questions?** (Teachers; we can't; only from God.)

● **What's good about asking questions like these?** (They stretch your brain; they help you find purpose.)

Say: **Asking tough questions is an important part of our development as Christians. One of the first important questions we ask is: "What's new life in Jesus all about?" In this lesson, we'll take a look at Jesus' answer to that question and what it means for our lives.**

TOWERS

Form groups of no more than six. Have groups each find a flat place to work, such as a table. Give groups each about 40 3x5 cards, and tell them to build 5-story towers out of their cards only. Explain that they may not tear or cut the cards. Tell them they have 10 minutes to complete their towers. After

ACTION AND REFLECTION
(10 to 15 minutes)

four minutes—or when people start getting frustrated—tell them you have tape to help hold their towers together.

Give the tape to the groups. After another five minutes—or when groups have completed their towers—have kids sit in a circle and discuss the activity.

Ask:

● **How did you initially feel about trying to build the towers? Why?** (It was frustrating because it kept falling down; it was easy, I've done this before.)

● **How did your feelings change when I offered the tape?** (I felt relieved; I was glad because I knew it could be done.)

● **Imagine your life is the tower you just built. What is the "tape" that makes it work?** (God's help; patience.)

● **How was getting tape in the middle of your frustration like getting a second wind or a new life?** (All of a sudden, I knew we could finish the tower; I had new confidence.)

● **What kind of changes does God bring about in your life when you accept God's tape—new life in Jesus?** (Things go better; I have more responsibility to God; my lifestyle changes; I think about other people more.)

● Say: **Jesus' message to Nicodemus in the Gospel of John clearly illustrates what happens when we accept new life in Christ. Next we'll examine how our lives change when we accept this gift.**

BIBLE APPLICATION
(10 to 15 minutes)

NEW LIFE

Make sure everyone has a Bible, a sheet of paper and a pencil. Have someone read aloud John 3:1-21. Then have teenagers each write on their paper how they might've felt had they been Nicodemus in this situation.

Form pairs. Have partners share what they wrote. Read aloud the following questions for partners to discuss.

Ask:

● **What was Jesus speaking about when he said Nicodemus would have to be "born again"?**

● **What does it mean to have a new "spiritual life"?**

● **How important is the message of John 3:16 for Christians? Explain.**

● **How do people change when they become Christians?**

Say: **Jesus' message to Nicodemus is also a message to each of us. When we become Christians, our spirits are "reborn" with Jesus at the center. But simply believing in God isn't enough. Being reborn implies a complete change in lifestyle.**

COMMITMENT
(5 to 10 minutes)

NEW-LIFE LOVE

Distribute the "New-Life Love" handout (p. 17) and pencils. Ask teenagers to answer the questions seriously, then meditate quietly on them. After five minutes, ask teenagers to tell what they wrote for one question if they feel comfortable doing so. Give everyone a chance to talk, but don't force anyone. Ask kids each to take their handout home and read it often.

☐ OPTION 1: LOVE AND RELATIONSHIPS

Have teenagers stand and form a circle. Say: **Sometimes we forget to acknowledge the importance of love in our relationship with God and our relationships with each other. During the next few minutes, go to each person in the room—one at a time. Look each person in the eyes, tell him or her that you care and what's your greatest hope for your relationship with him or her; for example: "I'm hopeful you and I will become good friends" or "I'm hopeful you'll enjoy being a part of this group."**

If you have a large group, limit the number of people kids talk to. After a few minutes, gather the group back into the circle. Close in prayer, thanking God for Jesus' message in John 3:1-21 and asking God to help kids live new lives according to God's will.

☐ OPTION 2: NEW-LIFE RESOLUTIONS

Have the group form a circle. Say: **We all have the potential to be strong Christians—living the new life Jesus taught about. And each of us already has strengths we can count on. One at a time, each of us will take a turn standing in the center of the circle. When someone steps into the circle, everyone else may call out strengths this person has that can help him or her be a strong Christian.**

Be sure each person has an opportunity to stand in the circle. Call out strengths you see for each person so teenagers each hear at least one positive thing; for example: a caring attitude, concern for others, patience, and love for God. After everyone has had a turn in the circle, close by saying together: **We resolve to use our strengths to live the new life Jesus called us to live.**

If You Still Have Time . . .

Love Stories—Form groups of two or three. Have kids talk about incidents in their lives when they really felt God's love. Ask them to discuss what happened and how they responded.

New Life Actions—Form groups of no more than four. Have groups brainstorm practical ways to live a new life as a Christian. Then gather groups together, and have them share their lists and discuss them.

Contract
AND READING GUIDE

Contract

I believe that reading the Bible is an important part of my faith development. I hereby agree to read through the entire book of John during the next four weeks. I further agree to faithfully attend all of the class sessions on John and, inasmuch as I am able, support and encourage others in my group to read this book.

Signed _____ Date_____

Outline

The following outline is designed to help you read through the book of John in four weeks. Read one or more segments each day and you'll have read the entire book in four weeks or less.

Segment	Passage (chapters and verses)	Title
☐ 1	1:1-42	Who Is This Person?
☐ 2	1:43—2:12	The Beginning
☐ 3	2:13-25	An Act of Rage
☐ 4	3:1-36	How Can This Be?
☐ 5	4:1-42	Encounter at Sychar
☐ 6	4:43—5:17	Miracles at Home
☐ 7	5:18-47	Who Is This Person?
☐ 8	6:1-40	Jesus Teaches the Masses
☐ 9	6:41-71	Hard Sayings
☐ 10	7:1-52	What People Are Saying
☐ 11	8:1-11	Judging Others
☐ 12	8:12-59	Fathers and Sons
☐ 13	9:1-41	Blind Men's Bluff
☐ 14	10:1-18	The Lord Is Our Shepherd
☐ 15	10:19-42	Temper, Temper
☐ 16	11:1—12:11	The Beginning of the End
☐ 17	12:12-50	One Last Public Word
☐ 18	13:1-20	How a Servant Leads
☐ 19	13:21-38	Some Betrayals
☐ 20	14:1-31	Hope for the Future
☐ 21	15:1-17	"I Am the Vine"
☐ 22	15:18—16:15	The Counselor Is Coming
☐ 23	16:16-33	Plain Talk
☐ 24	17:1-26	A Prayer for Friends
☐ 25	18:1-27	Busted and Betrayed
☐ 26	18:28—19:16	A Crash Due to Pilate Error
☐ 27	19:17—20:31	The Ultimate Comeback
☐ 28	21:1-25	Peter's Heart Is Resurrected

💙 New-Life Love 💙

One of the key ingredients of a new life with Christ is love. Take a few minutes to answer the following questions about the love you give and receive.

● How does it make you feel that God sent his son to die because he loves you?

● What can you do to show your love to God?

● How do others show their love for you? Be specific.

● What specific actions can you take to share your Christian love with others?

● What changes will you commit to make in your attitudes and behavior as you live a new life in Christ?

LESSON 2

WE'RE ALL SHEEP

Sheep without a shepherd wander aimlessly. They get lost. They get into trouble. Teenagers are like that too. Without a shepherd, they may walk into dangerous or difficult situations. But when teenagers become Christians, Jesus becomes their shepherd.

LESSON AIM

To help teenagers know what it means to be a part of Jesus' flock.

OBJECTIVES

Students will:
● identify themselves as a part of a community;
● understand how the "shepherd" leadership style works;
● learn how Jesus shepherds them; and
● feel good about the group they belong to.

BIBLE BASIS
JOHN 10:1-18
PSALM 23

Look up the following scriptures. Then read the background paragraphs to see how the passages relate to your senior highers.

In **John 10:1-18**, Jesus is discussing the Pharisees' ignorance concerning his mission.

In his analogy of the shepherd and the sheep, Jesus identifies himself as the Messiah. Many false messiahs had made the claim before Jesus came on the scene, so people were skeptical. Yet Jesus was worthy of this title because he was willing to lay down his life to see the "sheep" reach home safely.

There are many false messiahs vying for teenagers' allegiance today. And many teenagers' peers have given their allegiance to these messiahs of power, wealth and popularity. It's easy for teenagers to join the "flocks" of false messiahs. Yet as this scripture states, there really is only one shepherd—Jesus.

In **Psalm 23**, David describes the Lord as our shepherd. David's beautiful Psalm helps us understand no matter how bad things get, God still cares for us. David knew confidently that he could always turn to God—even after making mistakes.

Many of today's teenagers can't see beyond the immediate circumstances they're in. They think no one's watching out for them, and they have great difficulty seeing purpose and meaning in their lives. But by seeing how God cares for them—as David describes in Psalm 23—they can learn to feel a sense of peace and better understand a purpose in their busy lives.

THIS LESSON AT A GLANCE

Section	Minutes	What Students Will Do	Supplies
Opener (Option 1)	up to 5	**Secret Greetings**—Form groups based on the way they greet each other.	"Greeting Cards" hand-outs (p. 25), scissors
(Option 2)		**Group ID**—Determine a gesture or greeting to identify the class.	
Action and Reflection	10 to 15	**Sheep and Shepherd**—Experience what it feels like to be led by a shepherd.	Blindfolds
Bible Application	10 to 15	**How to Spot a Sheep**—Discover what the Bible says about being Jesus' sheep.	Tape, posterboard, markers, Bibles
Commitment	10 to 15	**How Do You Follow?**—Complete a handout and think about what they can do to be better "sheep."	"How Do You Follow?" handouts (p. 26), pencils, Bible
Closing (Option 1)	5 to 10	**Good Work, Sheep!**—Recognize each other's contributions to the group.	
(Option 2)		**Feeling Sheepish**—Say why they feel like they belong to the group.	

The Lesson

☐ OPTION 1: SECRET GREETINGS

Distribute a greeting card from the "Greeting Cards" hand-out (p. 25) to each person. Be sure to distribute the same amount of each card. Tell kids each to look at their card but not tell anyone else what's on it. Tell kids how many people are in each group. Then have kids each mill around the room and greet people according to the instructions on their card.

O P E N E R
(up to 5 minutes)

As they find people who use the same greeting, have kids form a group. Declare the first group that finds all its members the winning group.

Ask:

● **How did the winning group find their people first?** (They watched how people were greeting each other; they asked them.)

● **How comfortable were you with your method of greeting? Explain.** (Not very comfortable, because I looked stupid; I was uncomfortable, it was hard to do; very comfortable, it was fun.)

● **What does the way people greet each other say about them?** (It tells whether they're confident or shy; it helps you know if they're friendly or not.)

● **Why do people like to form groups or hang out with other people?** (They like to be social; they like to be around people.)

Say: **Humans are one of the most social species on the planet. You've probably noticed that people tend to hang out in groups when they're in public, or that there are many different types of groups and organizations in the world. Many groups have unique ways of identifying themselves. For example, scouting troops have easy-to-recognize uniforms; business people carry briefcases; students carry notebooks or schoolbooks. But what identifies Christians as a unique group? Today we'll dive into an examination of what Jesus means when he says we're like sheep.**

☐ OPTION 2: GROUP ID

Gather the class in the middle of the room, and say you're working on a new way for the class to identify itself. Say: **Imagine you're walking through a shopping mall and you see someone off in the distance who's a member of your Sunday school. What kind of gesture can you use to let him or her know you're members of the same group—other than just waving?**

Have kids each come up with their own gesture and demonstrate it for the class. Tell them they have too many gestures for one person to keep track of. Form groups of no more than four. Have groups each decide on a gesture they think would be best. Then have groups each present their gesture. Afterward, have kids vote on the gesture they like best.

Ask:

● **In your groups, how did you decide on the gesture you wanted to present?** (We were talked into it; it looked fun; it was easy to do; it was the goofiest one.)

● **Would you feel comfortable identifying yourself in public that way? Why or why not?** (No, I'd feel stupid; yes, it'd be fun; sure, it's original.)

● **Besides a unique greeting, what are ways people iden-**

tify themselves as being from a particular group? (The way they dress; the way they talk; how they act.)

Say: **Every group identifies its members in some way, and most try to be unique in doing it. For example, some groups wave; some salute; some rub noses; some shout at each other; some purse their lips; and some point. All these things are used to identify membership in a particular group. Christians are no different. We identify ourselves as different because of our relationship with Jesus. Today we're going to talk about Jesus' identification of his followers as sheep.**

SHEEP AND SHEPHERD

Ask for a volunteer, but don't explain what he or she will do. Gather the rest of the class on one side of the room. Create an obstacle course between the group and a designated area on the opposite side, using furniture and other materials in the room.

Tell the class: **You're going to walk from one side of the room to the other, but you're going to be blindfolded. So it'll be a little tougher than usual. To make things easier for you, keep saying "baa" like a sheep. This way, you'll find out where other people are. Our volunteer will serve as your "shepherd." This person will help you by gently nudging you in the right direction and calling out directions. The shepherd can't use hands or tell you anything except directions such as "over here" or "turn right." This activity will end when all of you are safely herded over to the "corral."**

Point out a place at the other end of the room to be the corral. Blindfold everyone but the shepherd, making sure blindfolded kids can't see. Then start the activity.

While this is going on, make things tougher for the kids by nudging them the wrong way, getting in their way and changing the course. If you have more than 12 people, you might want to try using two or more shepherds and corrals, and having the sheep identify themselves as belonging to their respective flocks by "baaing" differently.

After all the sheep have made it to the corral, ask:
● **What was it like to be a sheep?** (I felt helpless; confusing; aggravating; fun.)
● **What was it like to be a shepherd?** (I had power; I was needed; I was busy.)
● **How did the sheep feel about the shepherd?** (Dependent; grateful; ungrateful.)
● **How did you feel when you realized someone was turning you the wrong way?** (Angry; confused.)
● **How is being a Christian like being a sheep?** (We're dependent on Jesus; Christians will wander without God's direction.)
● **What does this activity teach us about our relation-**

ship with Jesus? (We're dependent on him; we can wander off if we want to; Jesus is gentle; there are obstacles; other people or things interfere.)

● **What specific things can we do to be better "sheep"?** (Listen to God more; follow God's directions; stay close to the rest of Jesus' flock.)

● **How is being turned the wrong way in the activity like being led away from our faith as Christians?** (People try to get us to do wrong things; sometimes we don't watch where we're going and end up doing something wrong.)

Say: **The Bible is our guidebook for how to act as sheep. Next we're going to discover how we can be the best sheep we can be for our shepherd.**

BIBLE APPLICATION
(10 to 15 minutes)

HOW TO SPOT A SHEEP

Tape a large sheet of posterboard to the wall. Give kids each a marker and a Bible. Say: **John was very concerned with the "flock" of believers he was a member of, and this concern showed up in everything he wrote. We can better understand what it means to belong to Jesus' flock by looking at what John had to say.**

Form five groups of one or more, and assign each group a chapter in 1 John. Have groups each look in their chapter for qualities or behaviors that describe a Christian sheep. Have groups write or draw something on the posterboard to express their discoveries. They can write a single word; compose a poem; draw a picture; or do anything else they think will get the point across.

While they're looking things up, write "How to Spot a Sheep" on the posterboard in big letters. Allow groups up to 10 minutes to read their chapters, discuss them, and write or draw on the posterboard. Then have groups each explain what they wrote or drew after everyone is done.

Have someone read aloud John 10:1-18.

● **According to Jesus' message in this passage, what does it mean to be Jesus' sheep?** (We're to love him and do his will; Jesus loves us and will lead us.)

● **Is it always easy being a sheep? Explain.** (Yes, I'm totally committed to God; no, sometimes I'm tempted to do wrong things.)

Say: **Jesus wants us to be his sheep. He wants us to live lives that make him proud to have us in his flock. What can we do specifically to be better followers? Let's take a few minutes to consider some ideas.**

COMMITMENT
(10 to 15 minutes)

HOW DO YOU FOLLOW?

Distribute a copy of the "How Do You Follow?" handout (p. 26) and a pencil to each person. Have kids each complete their handout. Assure them they won't have to reveal what they wrote.

Then ask:

● **How do you feel about being identified as one of Jesus' sheep? Explain.** (Good, I'm happy to be a Christian; uncomfortable, my friends pick on me; confused, I'm not sure what Jesus expects of me.)

● **How important is it that we, as Jesus' sheep, stick together? Explain.** (Very, because others will tempt us to do wrong; not at all, we need to be individuals.)

Have someone read aloud Psalm 23 while kids reflect on their completed handouts. Encourage kids to keep their handouts as reminders of ways they can become better sheep as they grow in faith.

☐ OPTION 1: GOOD WORK, SHEEP!

Form a circle. If you have more than 12 kids, form circles of six to 12.

Say: **Every group is made up of individuals who contribute something to it. Even the most unnoticeable sheep contribute something to the flock, and people are the same way.**

Now we'll stop and recognize the contributions everyone's been making to our group.

Starting with the person on your left, have kids each take a turn quickly walking around the circle. As each person walks around the circle, have group members call out things they appreciate about that person's contributions to the group, such as: "You have great ideas" or "Your smile keeps us happy." When a person completes his or her circle, have the next person begin. Be sure every person receives at least one message of appreciation.

Continue until your turn is over, then have a short prayer thanking God for the other members of Jesus' flock and what they contribute to group members' lives.

☐ OPTION 2: FEELING SHEEPISH

Have the class stand in a circle. Say: **We all act out our belonging to this group in some important way. Everyone's contribution to what we do here—no matter how small it appears to be—helps make this group great. We're going to go around the circle, starting with the person on my right, and have you each say one thing you do that identifies you as a part of this group. Begin by saying "I feel sheepish when I . . . " then complete the sentence. For example, someone might say: "I feel sheepish when I participate in discussions" or "I feel sheepish when I play games with the group." After you say what makes you feel like you belong, everyone else should say in unison, "We're glad you're part of our flock."**

Go around the circle once and conclude with a prayer, focusing on the unity of your flock and the love of your shepherd.

CLOSING
(5 to 10 minutes)

If You Still Have Time . . .

Sheep Inspection—Make up a list of questions such as "If you saw someone drop a dollar on the sidewalk and walk away, would you pick it up and keep it or try to return it?" Then ask a group member to answer one question. If the rest of the group thinks the answer he or she gives is in line with Jesus' desires for his flock, have them respond by saying "baa" as if they were sheep. If they think the answer isn't in line with Jesus' desire for his flock, have them respond with "moo."

Church Wool Check—Have group members talk about the type of "wool" the group produces—what things they do to benefit others. List these things on newsprint or the other side of the posterboard from How to Spot a Sheep. After discussing these items, have kids create a slogan that describes the group's wool-producing capabilities.

Greeting Cards

Photocopy this page, and cut apart the greeting cards. Be sure to make at least three copies of each card you choose. If you have a small group, you may only use copies of two or three different cards. If you have a large group, you may use copies of all the cards.

Greeting Card

When you greet someone, don't say anything. Wait for the other person to speak first. Then respond by saying, "Nice to meet you."

Greeting Card

Walk up and aggressively shake hands with the people you greet. Say, "Hello, my name is _____. Pleased to meet you."

Greeting Card

Walk up sheepishly to each person you greet and in a meek little voice say, "Hi."

Greeting Card

Greet each person with a "secret handshake" you make up. Make it really strange. For example, you might walk up to someone, swing your arms in circles, pat your head, touch your toes and then shake the person's hand.

Greeting Card

Greet each person with a "high five" (slapping hands together about head-high).

Greeting Card

Greet each person by asking, "What's new with you?"

What can you do to be one of Jesus' sheep? Take a few minutes to complete this handout. Then commit to taking action on your insights during the coming weeks.

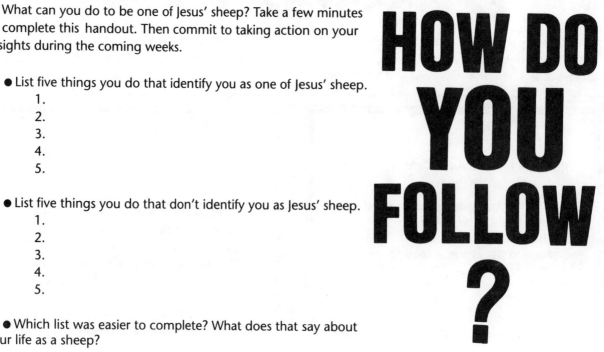

- List five things you do that identify you as one of Jesus' sheep.
    1.
    2.
    3.
    4.
    5.

- List five things you do that don't identify you as Jesus' sheep.
    1.
    2.
    3.
    4.
    5.

- Which list was easier to complete? What does that say about your life as a sheep?

- Look at your second list. How can you change these things around so they reflect your life as Jesus' sheep? List ideas for each one.

    1.
    2.
    3.
    4.
    5.

- Here are some areas you can develop to become a better sheep. Next to each one, list one or two specific ways you can improve this area in your life.
        Reading the Bible:

        Spending time with Christian friends:

        Praying:

        Serving others:

        Learning from other Christians:

THE VINE WE CLING TO

It's easy to describe Jesus as the shepherd and Christians as sheep. The imagery of a shepherd taking care of sheep is a clear one. But to describe Christians with that imagery alone would be insufficient. Sheep have very few responsibilities. But Christians—as they respond to Jesus' love—have many. Teenagers need to see what it means to live as Jesus' branches.

To help teenagers learn about a Christian's responsibilities.

Students will:
● **examine a Christian's role in sharing God's love;**
● **consider traits that make good followers of Jesus; and**
● **discuss the importance of "bearing fruit" as Christians.**

Look up the following scriptures. Then read the background paragraphs to see how the passages relate to your senior highers.

In **Isaiah 5:1-7,** the prophet describes God's disappointment with the people of Israel.

God had high hopes for Israel. But the people disappointed God. As a result, God decided to tear down the relationship that had gone so badly. As we know now, God had such high hopes for this relationship that he could never abandon the Israelites. Instead, God restored the relationship and broadened it by sending Jesus.

Teenagers, like everyone else, enter relationships with certain expectations of others. When a friend doesn't live up to those expectations, the relationship often disintegrates. But Jesus will always live up to his promises. Teenagers need

LESSON AIM

OBJECTIVES

BIBLE BASIS
ISAIAH 5:1-7
JOHN 15:1-17

to be responsible for their relationship with Jesus. Teenagers also need to understand the responsibility they have to be fruitful in their relationships with others.

In **John 15:1-17,** Jesus discusses the pattern of life he wants Christians to follow.

Jesus tells us here how he wants his followers to be extensions of him in the world. He also stresses the importance of producing fruit in the world by demonstrating love toward everyone.

For many of today's teenagers, maintaining enduring relationships is difficult. Many pressures force them apart from certain friends, and some kids may even have trouble knowing who their friends *are*! The directions Jesus gives here help kids understand how to maintain healthy, enduring relationships.

THIS LESSON AT A GLANCE

Section	Minutes	What Students Will Do	Supplies
Opener (Option 1)	5 to 10	**Newspaper Creation**—Create something from newspapers and discuss the importance of guidelines and effort.	Newspapers, tape
(Option 2)		**The Big Sale**—Try to sell an object.	Worthless item
Action and Reflection	10 to 15	**The Vine**—Play a game to demonstrate the responsibilities of Christians.	Buckets, water, paper cups, paper towels
Bible Application	15 to 20	**The Branches**—Discuss what the Bible says about bearing fruit.	Bibles, tape, rope, "Fruit of the Vine" handouts (p. 33), pencils, clothespins or tape
Commitment	5 to 10	**Fruit or Nuts?**—Complete a handout and discuss what it means to be fruitful.	"Fruit or Nuts?" handouts (p. 34), pencils
Closing (Option 1)	5 to 10	**Better Branches**—Determine traits each person has that make him or her a good follower of Jesus.	Markers or pencils, vine from The Branches
(Option 2)		**Congratulations**—Describe ways each person bears fruit.	Copies of "Congratulations" box (p. 32), pencils

The Lesson

☐ OPTION 1: NEWSPAPER CREATION

Bring a small stack of newspapers and a couple of rolls of tape into class with you. Toss them on the floor in the center of the room, and tell the class: **I'm going to leave the room and give you five minutes to use these materials to make anything you want. You can make this a team project, or you can each make something of your own. Whatever you decide to do, you only have five minutes, so go!**

Leave the room. After five minutes, come back and see what they made, making sure to compliment them no matter what they did. If they didn't build anything, ask why; then skip down to the third question, "How did you feel about this activity?" Continue on from there.

Then ask:
● **How did you decide what to build?** (We were talked into it; we discussed ideas, then picked one.)
● **How easy was this for you? Explain.** (Very easy, I like being creative; not very easy, I didn't know what to do; I didn't understand why we had to do it.)
● **How did you feel about this activity?** (Confused; fine.)
● **How would this activity have been different had I told you specifically what to create?** (It would've been better; it wouldn't be any different.)
● **How much effort did you put into this project? Explain.** (Not much, we didn't know what to do; a lot, we wanted to make something great.)

Say: **If we don't have guidelines for a project or activity, we often don't do anything. Or we do something with only half our effort. In this activity, no guidelines were given. Clear instructions are important for projects. They're also important as we try to live as Jesus' sheep. Jesus has given us guidelines for living as Christians. Today we're going to examine some of those guidelines.**

☐ OPTION 2: THE BIG SALE

Bring in something from your home you don't need. Find the most useless piece of junk you can, even if that means raiding a trash can! Give the class members the object, and say: **I want you to take this object and find a way to sell it to the first person I bring in the room. You can tell him or her anything you want. Whatever money you collect goes to the youth program. You only have three minutes to complete the sale. I'll go out and find somebody. While I'm gone, plan your sales pitch.**

Bring in someone from another class to participate in the

activity. Or arrange for an adult to visit your class. Don't explain the activity, just say the kids are going to ask a few questions. Tell the person he or she may leave at any time during the activity.

Allow at least two minutes for the class to work up a good sales pitch before bringing the person into the room. Allow up to two minutes for kids to present their pitch. After the volunteer leaves, ask:

● **How do you feel about this exercise?** (Happy; nervous; disappointed; confused.)

● **What went right—or wrong—with your sales pitch?** (We overdid it; we had a bad product; the volunteer didn't play along; we had a great sales pitch.)

● **What was the difference in the value of the item before and after you tried to sell it? Explain.** (It was worth a little bit more after trying to convince the volunteer of the item's value; it didn't change.)

Say: **Anything can have value if you try hard enough to find that value. The item you tried to sell was given value because you had a goal of selling it. Our faith has value because we can live it and give it to others. Today we're going to discover how developing our relationship with Jesus can make our Christian faith more valuable to us.**

ACTION AND REFLECTION
(10 to 15 minutes)

THE VINE

Bring in a bucket of water, an empty bucket and one empty cup for each person. Place the bucket with the water in it on the opposite side of the room from the empty bucket. Have the class line up between the two buckets with you in the middle and everyone holding a cup.

Tell the class: **We're going to take the water out of this bucket and put it into the bucket at the other end of the line. The object is to move as much water as possible from the full bucket into the empty bucket. To do this, the person closest to the water bucket will take a cup, dip it into the bucket and then pour it into the next person's cup. This person will pour it into the *next* person's cup, and so on, until the last person pours it into the bucket at the end.**

Keep the water flowing as smoothly as possible. When the empty bucket is about half-filled, start taking large sips out of your cup as the water goes by. When the first bucket is empty, stop the activity. Have paper towels available for clean-up.

Ask:

● **What went well in this exercise?** (We completed the task; we didn't spill much.)

● **What hindered our progress?** (You kept drinking the water; people kept spilling the water.)

● **How did you feel when someone drank or spilled the water? Explain.** (Angry, he or she wasn't careful; frustrated, I was doing my job so why couldn't everyone?)

● **If you were to look at the first bucket as Jesus and the other bucket as non-Christians, what might the water represent?** (God's love; Jesus' teachings; the Bible.)

● **What does this activity say about our roles as Christians?** (We're responsible to get Jesus' love to people; some of us take Jesus' love in but don't produce anything.)

Say: **When we become Christians, we accept not only Jesus' love but also Jesus' command for us to share that love with others.**

THE BRANCHES

Have someone read aloud Isaiah 5:1-7 and John 15:1-17. Ask:

● **What do these passages suggest about our relationship with Jesus and our relationships with others?** (We're to lean on Jesus for strength; Jesus wants us to share his love with others; we're Jesus' branches.)

● **What does Jesus mean when he says he's the vine and we're the branches?** (Jesus is the source of all life and love; Jesus is the center of our lives.)

● **What can we learn from Jesus' teaching in John 15:1-17 to help us be better followers?** (Rely on Jesus; show love to others.)

● **What does it mean to "bear fruit"?** (To share Jesus with others; to do good things for people; to love other people.)

Tape a thin rope to the ceiling or high on a wall. Form groups of no more than five. Distribute copies of the "Fruit of the Vine" handout (p. 33) and pencils to each group.

Say: **Being Jesus' branches requires certain things of us. Many of these are described in the book of James. In your groups, read aloud James 3—4 and determine actions, attitudes and attributes associated with being Jesus' branches. List each of these actions, attitudes or attributes in the branch on one of the handouts.**

Allow groups up to five minutes to read James 3—4 and write in the handouts. Then give groups clothespins or tape to attach their handouts to the rope. Have kids walk around the "vine" and silently read the words on the branches.

Say: **Without the branches we added, this vine couldn't produce fruit. Yet producing fruit is an important responsibility we have as Christians. Now we'll think of ways to be fruitful in specific situations.**

FRUIT OR NUTS?

Give a "Fruit or Nuts?" handout (p. 34) and a pencil to each teenager. Have teenagers each complete their handout.

Then ask:

● **What does it mean to be fruitful?** (To tell others about Christ; to be nice to people; to live as a good Christian; to invite others to church.)

● **How easy is it to live out fruitful behavior? Explain.**
(It's tough, sometimes I don't know what to do; it's easy, I work on it all the time.)

● **What can we do to make our lives more fruitful?** (Pray more; help each other; think before we act.)

Say: **To be fruitful we need to be sure our branches are strong and filled with Jesus' love and guidance. Take 20 seconds to silently pray for God to give you attitudes, actions and behaviors that'll help you bear fruit.**

Allow 20 seconds of silence before moving on.

☐ OPTION 1: BETTER BRANCHES

Give kids each a marker or a pencil. Say: **We all have traits like those listed on the branches of our vine. Look around at the people in this room, and think about the items listed on our branches. Then go up to the vine, and write each person's name on a branch that describes one of his or her strong traits. You can use the same trait for more than one person.**

Afterward, have kids silently walk around and read where people wrote their names. Thank each person for the fruit he or she produces. Close with a prayer thanking God for giving us Jesus as our "vine."

☐ OPTION 2: CONGRATULATIONS

Give a copy of the "Congratulations" box and a pencil to each group member. Have people each write their name in the blank. Collect the papers with the boxes on them, shuffle them thoroughly and pass them out. Make sure people don't get their own paper. Ask kids not to say whose paper they have.

Have teenagers each complete the sentence on the paper they hold. Encourage kids to be honest and positive in what they write. Then collect the papers and return them to their original owners.

Close with a prayer thanking God for the fruit this group produces.

CLOSING
(5 to 10 minutes)

Congratulations

Congratulations, _____,
you bear fruit when you . . .

If You Still Have Time . . .

Fruit of the Week—Have the group vote and award a piece of fruit with the words "Fruit of the Week" written on it to whoever they decide has been the most fruitful member over the past week.

Vine Clippings—Get a vine or a branch to represent a vine. Cut a 2-inch clipping from it for each person in your class. Tell kids to use the vines or branches as reminders to help them be better "branches." Ask kids to discuss practical ways they can help each other serve God better.

FRUiT OF THE ViNE

FRUIT OR NUTS?

Read each situation below. Next to the fruit, write a response that would bear fruit—one that fits with Jesus' teaching in John 15:1-17. Next to the nuts, write a response that wouldn't bear fruit—one that goes against Jesus' teaching.

Situation	Response
The soft drink machine around the corner is broken and gives you two cans for the price of one.	
Your friends tell you they've found a way to sneak into movies. They've asked you to come with them to a movie you really want to see.	
Your friends are picking on a new kid at school. You notice no one sits with her at lunch.	
You find a small bag of pills in the school library.	
You have a paper due tomorrow, but your friends want you to go to the mall with them tonight. Your parents will let you go, but your teacher counts off for late papers.	
A member of your Sunday school shows up at school with a new portable stereo—and you recognize it as the one stolen from the Sunday school room.	
Your Sunday school teacher asks you to do something that sounds really stupid.	

FOLLOW ME

Jesus taught many things to his disciples. But one of the most important lessons he taught came at the end of his time on Earth, following his Resurrection. When Jesus told Peter to "feed my sheep," he was telling all Christians to serve others and take his message into the world. Teenagers need to see the importance of this message and how it relates to their lives.

To help teenagers understand Jesus' command to "feed my sheep."

LESSON AIM

Students will:
- see how Jesus' message to "feed my sheep" applies to them;
- learn what it means to follow Jesus; and
- commit to do Jesus' work in the world.

OBJECTIVES

Look up the following scriptures. Then read the background paragraphs to see how the passages relate to your senior highers.

BIBLE BASIS
MARK 16:15-20
JOHN 21:15-19

In **Mark 16:15-20,** Jesus tells his disciples to go out into the world and preach the good news.

This passage illustrates the importance of taking Jesus' teachings seriously. Jesus commanded the disciples to take what he'd taught them to all the people of the world. And as it says in verse 20, the Lord continued to work with them in all they did.

It's not always easy to be a Christian. Teenagers may be ridiculed or picked on because of their faith. But as this passage illustrates, teenagers can live out their faith confidently, knowing that Jesus will work with them in all they do—just as he did with the disciples.

In **John 21:15-19,** Jesus tells Peter to "feed my sheep."
This passage illustrates Jesus' reinstatement of Peter as a beloved disciple. In stark contrast to Peter's earlier denials of

Christ, Peter three times affirms Jesus' question: "Do you love me?" But the key to this conversation follows Peter's response to Jesus.

Jesus' command to "feed my sheep" is an important message for all of Christ's disciples. If we love Jesus, we're to live out his Word and feed others with it. This is an important lesson for senior highers, who may answer Jesus' question affirmatively—as Peter did—but not fully understand what that means for their lives.

THIS LESSON AT A GLANCE

Section	Minutes	What Students Will Do	Supplies
Opener (Option 1)	5 to 10	**Feeding Time**—Play a game and discuss the importance of knowing how to follow Jesus' teachings.	Buckets, marshmallows or crumpled paper balls
(Option 2)		**New Foods**—Create imaginary foods that have unusual nutritional values.	Newsprint, markers
Action and Reflection	10 to 15	**Follow Me**—Experience how following a leader is important to completing a task.	
Bible Application	10 to 15	**Feed My Sheep**—Learn what the Bible says about sharing Jesus' teachings.	Bibles, posterboard, markers
Commitment	10 to 15	**Nourishment**—Determine ways to give and get nourishment from Jesus' teachings.	"Nourishment" handouts (p. 42), pencils
Closing (Option 1)	up to 5	**Moving Forward**—Tell things they appreciate about each other.	Ball of yarn
(Option 2)		**Taking a Step**—Describe teachings that are meaningful.	

The Lesson

OPENER
(5 to 10 minutes)

☐ OPTION 1: FEEDING TIME

Form teams of no more than six. Give teams each a bucket and a supply of marshmallows. Or you may use crumpled-up paper balls. Have teams each form a circle around their bucket, standing at least 5 feet away from the bucket. Have teenagers each grab a supply of marshmallows.

Say: **Today we're going to begin our lesson by playing a game called Feeding Time. The object of the game is simple—to "feed" your bucket more marshmallows than** any other team. You do this by tossing the marshmallows into the bucket. **Once you toss a marshmallow, you can't pick it up again. So toss carefully.**

Tell at least one team to turn around and face away from the bucket before starting. If you have more than three teams, have half the teams face away from their buckets and the other half face their buckets. Tell kids on the teams facing away that they must toss the marshmallows over their heads, without turning around to look at the bucket. Kids will probably complain that the game isn't fair. Let them complain, but don't let groups turn around.

On "go," begin the game. After all the marshmallows have been thrown, call time. Count the number of marshmallows in each bucket and declare the winning team.

Ask:

● **How did you feel if you were on a team that was facing away from the buckets?** (It was unfair; uncomfortable; upset.)

● **Which teams had the best chance of winning? Explain.** (The ones who faced the buckets, because they could see what they were doing.)

● **How successful were the team(s) who tossed the marshmallows blindly? Explain.** (Not very successful, they couldn't see what they were doing; moderately successful, their tosses were wild.)

● **How is tossing the marshmallows blindly like the way some people try to do God's work?** (They don't know what they're doing; they don't understand how to do God's work.)

● **How important is it to know Jesus' teachings in order to do God's work? Explain.** (Very important, you need to know what you're talking about; important, you need to know what you believe before you tell someone else about Jesus.)

Say: **Jesus wants Christians to follow him and share his good news with others. But sharing the good news with others isn't always easy. Sometimes it's like tossing marshmallows blindly into a bucket. But by learning more about Jesus' teachings, we can learn how to feed Jesus' sheep.**

☐ OPTION 2: NEW FOODS

Form groups of no more than five. Give groups each a sheet of newsprint and markers. Have groups each develop one imaginary food item that has exceptional nutritional value and tastes good too. For example, kids might create a fruit that has every vitamin and mineral, and also helps people think more clearly at school. Then have them each design an ad describing the benefits of their new food.

Say: **As you create your new food, remember to consider what it tastes like, what it looks like, what it smells like and what it can do for you. The benefits don't have to be only physical; they can be emotional, intellectual**

and spiritual. Make this food something that meets many needs.

Allow five minutes for groups to create their new foods. Then have groups each present their ad and describe their food to the rest of the kids.

Ask:

● **What did you notice about the kinds of foods people designed?** (They sounded great; one seemed really weird.)

● **Would you eat these foods if they existed? Explain.** (Yes, they'd solve all my problems; no, they look too weird.)

● **How are these foods like the spiritual food we get from our relationship with God?** (Our relationship, like these foods, provides for our needs; they help us grow.)

Say: **Just as the foods we created would do great things for us, the spiritual food we receive from studying Jesus' teachings can do great things. The more spiritual food we take in, the more we grow closer to God. But Jesus doesn't just want only us to grow spiritually. He also wants us to share our spiritual food with others. Today we're going to find out what it means to follow Jesus' command to "feed my sheep."**

ACTION AND REFLECTION
(10 to 15 minutes)

FOLLOW ME

Form three groups. Have groups each designate a leader. Tell the leaders to lead their groups around the building while the group discusses what it means to follow Jesus. Set a specific time for groups to return. You may need to limit kids' movement to a small part of the church. While they march around, go up to one of the groups, and tell the kids to follow their leader only half of the time. Then tell another group to split up and stop following its leader altogether. Be sure at least one group stays together the whole time. Have groups continue their walking discussions for about six or seven minutes. Then tell the groups to return to the meeting room and form a circle. If you have a small class, have the same group repeat the activity three times: once staying together all the time; once staying together part of the time; and once where the group stops following the leader altogether.

Have groups each briefly share what they talked about during their walk.

Ask:

● **How did you feel if your group didn't stay together for the discussion?** (Frustrated; angry; it didn't bother me.)

● **How is that like the feeling Jesus might have when people don't follow him?** (It's the same; he probably feels disappointed.)

● **How important was following the leader in completing the assignment of talking about what it means to follow Jesus?** (Very important; somewhat important.)

● **How is following Jesus like following the leader in this exercise?** (When we don't follow, we miss out on important things; when we follow, we can talk with Jesus.)

● **What does it mean to follow Jesus?** (To do things Jesus would want us to do; to read the Bible; to share Jesus' teachings with others.)

Say: **After his Resurrection from the dead, Jesus appeared to the disciples and gave them specific instructions. Next we'll take a look at what he told his followers and what that means for us.**

FEED MY SHEEP

Form groups of no more than five. Give groups each a Bible, a sheet of posterboard and markers. Have groups each read aloud Mark 16:15-20 and John 21:15-19. Have them discuss Jesus' message in both passages.

Have groups each discuss the following questions:

● **What does it mean to "go into all the world and preach the good news to all creation"?**

● **How does this command make you feel?**

● **How do you feel, knowing that Jesus will be with you as you preach the good news?**

● **How do you feel about Jesus asking you to "feed my sheep"?**

● **As Christians, what's our responsibility to preach the good news?**

● **How can we follow Jesus?**

Have groups each design a poster describing the message of these passages. Encourage kids to be creative. Allow groups up to 10 minutes to create their posters. Then have groups each present and explain their poster to the rest of the class.

Ask:

● **How do you feel about the messages of these posters?** (I'm challenged by them; I'm scared by them; I'm excited about them.)

NOURISHMENT

Say: **Jesus' command to Peter was to "feed my lambs." But Jesus wasn't just talking to Peter; he's talking to us too.**

Form pairs. Have partners complete the "Nourishment" handout (p. 42) together and briefly discuss the questions at the bottom of the handout.

Form a circle and have kids each share one thing they listed in the Feeding Time section of the handout.

Check back with kids about how they're doing reading the book of John. Suggest ways group members can help one another fulfill their commitment. For example, have a "reading party" at church for kids to read and discuss the book of John.

BIBLE APPLICATION
(10 to 15 minutes)

COMMITMENT
(10 to 15 minutes)

Table Talk

The Table Talk activity in this course helps senior highers discuss the Gospel of John with their parents.

If you choose to use the Table Talk activity, this is a good time to show students the "Table Talk" handout (p. 43). Ask them to spend time with their parents completing it.

Before kids leave, give them each the "Table Talk" handout to take home, or tell them you'll be sending it to their parents.

Or use the Table Talk idea found in the Bonus Ideas (p. 46) for a meeting based on the handout.

CLOSING
(up to 5 minutes)

☐ OPTION 1: MOVING FORWARD

Remain in a circle. Say: **Jesus taught his disciples many things in the Gospel of John. And each of his teachings can help us become better disciples today. As we go from this lesson, let's commit to move forward toward the kind of life Jesus wants for us. And as we move forward, let's encourage one another to grow in faith.**

Take a ball of yarn, and hold the loose end. Say: **As our closing, we're going to each say something we appreciate about another group member's strengths and abilities. I'll say something I appreciate about someone, then toss the ball of yarn to him or her. Then this person will say something about another person and, while holding the yarn taut, toss the ball to that person. We'll do this until everyone has had the yarn at least once.**

Be sensitive to people who don't get the ball of yarn, and toss it to them if you have the chance. While the web of yarn is still intact, close with prayer, thanking God for the relevant and important teachings Jesus gave in the Gospel of John.

☐ OPTION 2: TAKING A STEP

Have teenagers stand side by side in a line along the wall, facing the middle of the room. Say: **Jesus taught us many things in the Gospel of John. But none of those teachings are meaningful unless we act on them.**

Have group members each describe one of Jesus' teachings that's meaningful to them. After each person shares, have everyone take one small step forward. After each person has shared, say: **Just as we took one step forward as someone described Jesus' teaching, let us commit to moving forward in our walks of faith—striving to follow Jesus' teachings in all that we do.**

Thank each person for something he or she shared during the past four weeks. Begin by saying: " (name), I appreciate your contributions to this class. I'm glad you shared . . . " For example, you might thank kids for sharing personal stories, helping out with activities or being involved in discussions. Then have one or two volunteers close in prayer.

If You Still Have Time . . .

Feeding Friends—Form groups of no more than five. Have groups each brainstorm ways to share their faith with friends. Ask groups to each create a skit demonstrating one of these ways. Then have groups each perform their skit for the rest of the group.

Course Reflection—Form a circle. Ask students to reflect on the past four lessons. Have them take turns completing the following sentences:

- Something I learned in this course was . . .
- If I could tell my friends about this course, I'd say . . .
- Something I'll do differently because of this course is . . .

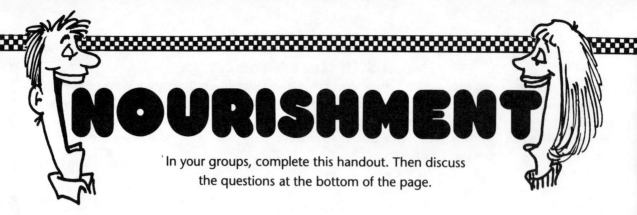

NOURISHMENT

In your groups, complete this handout. Then discuss
the questions at the bottom of the page.

Feeding Time

- List five specific ways you can fulfill Jesus' wishes by feeding his lambs:
    1.
    2.
    3.
    4.
    5.
- What three things can you do to keep up your own spiritual nourishment?
    1.
    2.
    3.
- Name three people you can count on for spiritual guidance and strength:
    1.
    2.
    3.

Food for Thought

- If you'd seen Jesus after his Resurrection—as the disciples did—how would you feel?
- What is the importance of Jesus' Resurrection for you?
- Is it always easy to follow Jesus? Explain.
- How do you think Peter felt when Jesus told him to "feed my sheep"?
- What one thing will you commit to do this week to feed Jesus' sheep?

Table Talk

To the Parent: We've just finished a senior high course at church called *The Gospel of John: Jesus' Teachings*. We'd like you and your teenager to spend some time discussing the topics we raised in the class. Use this "Table Talk" page to help you do that.

Parent and senior higher

Complete the following statements:
● To me, new life in Christ means . . .
● If Jesus were here, he'd tell me . . .
● John's Gospel is important because . . .
● A Christian's responsibilities include . . .
● Jesus' teachings are important to me because . . .

Together, read John 3:1-21; 10:1-18; 15:1-17; and 21:15-19. If you lived when Jesus was teaching and preaching, how would you respond to his teachings on:
● a spiritual life?
● being "born again"?
● what it means to be a branch of Jesus' vine?
● what it means to follow Jesus?

Describe a time when . . .
● you learned something important about your faith.
● someone helped you understand more about Jesus' teachings.

Take a minute to pray together, silently. Thank God for Jesus' teachings.

BONUS IDEAS

Jesus' Teachings Talk Show—Have a meeting where the whole congregation participates in a talk show about Jesus' teachings in John. Ask outgoing volunteers to play the hosts for the meeting. During the show, have volunteers ask congregation members how they feel about specific teachings in John. Spend an hour or so with your teenagers preparing good questions for the event. Then advertise it to your church. Include a time of refreshments following the talk show. This is a good way to help increase visibility of your group in the church.

Bible Study—Meet with interested kids once a week for a few months and dive into an in-depth study of the Gospel of John. Help kids see how John's Gospel differs from the first three. You might want to invite a variety of age groups to participate in this study.

"Dear God . . . "—Have group members each write a letter to God telling how they feel about Jesus' teachings. Ask them to express their joys, fears and doubts about what they learned in this course.

The Wave—Have the group invent a greeting that helps identify them as Jesus' flock. Have kids use it frequently. Be sure to teach it to new group members.

Jesus in Song—Have kids find hymns, choruses or contemporary Christian songs that describe Jesus' teachings. Have a meeting where kids discuss the songs and rate them according to appropriateness of message, quality of music and other factors.

We Want Ewe—Have your group members hold a strategy session where they work out creative and positive ways they can bring people who've not come to church lately back to the "flock." Suggest ideas such as creating a flier to promote the group, writing letters or making phone calls.

Don't Be a Nut!—Have kids make pocket-size cards that say "Don't be a Nut!" on them, along with the text of John 15:16-17. Encourage kids to keep these cards as a reminder to be fruitful in their walk with Christ.

What Would Jesus Do?—Have kids each complete the "What Would Jesus Do?" handout (p. 47) and discuss it in groups of no more than five.

MEETINGS AND MORE

Table Talk—Use the "Table Talk" handout (p. 43) as the basis for a parents and teenagers' meeting. Have parents and teenagers discuss the topics on the handout. Then have kids lead parents in their favorite activities from the four-week course. Include crowdbreakers, fun games, refreshments, discussion and worship. For crowdbreaker and game ideas, check out *Quick Crowdbreakers and Games for Youth Groups* (Group Books).

PARTY PLEASER

Group Dinner—Invite your class members and their friends to a dinner. Play games that emphasize working together as a group, such as volleyball; relays; Twister; or Win, Lose or Draw. Talk about the importance of teamwork. Include a time to discuss how the group is like or unlike Jesus' disciples.

RETREAT IDEAS

Bridging the Gap—Take your kids on a retreat that uses the theme of bridge-building. Structure your sessions to focus on the steps involved in building a bridge, such as: measuring the gap; making plans; laying a foundation; building the bridge; and opening it for business. Include activities where kids actually build a bridge out of newspapers and tape, or out of their bodies. Have kids create a "Blueprint" showing the state of their relationships with each other. And close with a service of reconciliation.

Wool-Gathering—In this retreat, focus on activities that stress group identity, using the sheep theme from "We're All Sheep." Form "flocks" instead of groups, and let kids each take a turn being a shepherd for their group. Use this retreat to help kids discover what makes their group unique.

Include several active games that pit flocks against each other. Also do large group exercises that focus on identity-building within the group. For fun, have a group photo taken on this retreat. Have the photo enlarged and placed in your Sunday school or youth room.

WHAT WOULD JESUS DO?

For each of the following situations, write what you think Jesus would do or say if he were in the situation described. Skim through the Gospel of John and read Jesus' teachings to help you know what to write.

What would Jesus do if ...
- someone was picking on a girl at school because she was a Christian?

- an elderly couple needed help fixing up their house?

- two kids were about to start a fight?

- someone was selling drugs at school?

- a family needed money to pay a bill?

- a teenager was cheating at school?

What would Jesus say to ...
- a depressed person?

- someone who ran away from home?

- a drug addict or alcoholic?

- a person who didn't believe in God?

- someone who needed a boost of self-confidence?

- people who say they're Christians, but don't act like Christians?

What would Jesus say to you about your relationship with him?

What can you learn from all these answers?

CURRICULUM REORDER—TOP PRIORITY

Order now to prepare for your upcoming Sunday school classes, youth ministry meetings, and weekend retreats! Each book includes all teacher and student materials—plus photocopiable handouts—for any size class . . . for just $8.99 each!

FOR SENIOR HIGH:

1 & 2 Corinthians: Christian Discipleship, ISBN 1-55945-230-7

Angels, Demons, Miracles & Prayer, ISBN 1-55945-235-8

Changing the World, ISBN 1-55945-236-6

Christians in a Non-Christian World, ISBN 1-55945-224-2

Christlike Leadership, ISBN 1-55945-231-5

Communicating With Friends, ISBN 1-55945-228-5

Counterfeit Religions, ISBN 1-55945-207-2

Dating Decisions, ISBN 1-55945-215-3

Dealing With Life's Pressures, ISBN 1-55945-232-3

Deciphering Jesus' Parables, ISBN 1-55945-237-4

Exodus: Following God, ISBN 1-55945-226-9

Exploring Ethical Issues, ISBN 1-55945-225-0

Faith for Tough Times, ISBN 1-55945-216-1

Forgiveness, ISBN 1-55945-223-4

Getting Along With Parents, ISBN 1-55945-202-1

Getting Along With Your Family, ISBN 1-55945-233-1

The Gospel of John: Jesus' Teachings, ISBN 1-55945-208-0

Hazardous to Your Health: AIDS, Steroids & Eating Disorders, ISBN 1-55945-200-5

Is Marriage in Your Future?, ISBN 1-55945-203-X

Jesus' Death & Resurrection, ISBN 1-55945-211-0

The Joy of Serving, ISBN 1-55945-210-2

Knowing God's Will, ISBN 1-55945-205-6

Life After High School, ISBN 1-55945-220-X

Making Good Decisions, ISBN 1-55945-209-9

Money: A Christian Perspective, ISBN 1-55945-212-9

Movies, Music, TV & Me, ISBN 1-55945-213-7

Overcoming Insecurities, ISBN 1-55945-221-8

Psalms, ISBN 1-55945-234-X

Real People, Real Faith: Amy Grant, Joni Eareckson Tada, Dave Dravecky, Terry Anderson, ISBN 1-55945-238-2

Responding to Injustice, ISBN 1-55945-214-5

Revelation, ISBN 1-55945-229-3

School Struggles, ISBN 1-55945-201-3

Sex: A Christian Perspective, ISBN 1-55945-206-4

Today's Lessons From Yesterday's Prophets, ISBN 1-55945-227-7

Turning Depression Upside Down, ISBN 1-55945-135-1

What Is the Church?, ISBN 1-55945-222-6

Who Is God?, ISBN 1-55945-218-8

Who Is Jesus?, ISBN 1-55945-219-6

Who Is the Holy Spirit?, ISBN 1-55945-217-X

Your Life as a Disciple, ISBN 1-55945-204-8

FOR JUNIOR HIGH/MIDDLE SCHOOL:

Accepting Others: Beyond Barriers & Stereotypes, ISBN 1-55945-126-2

Advice to Young Christians: Exploring Paul's Letters, ISBN 1-55945-146-7

Applying the Bible to Life, ISBN 1-55945-116-5

Becoming Responsible, ISBN 1-55945-109-2

Bible Heroes: Joseph, Esther, Mary & Peter, ISBN 1-55945-137-8

Boosting Self-Esteem, ISBN 1-55945-100-9

Building Better Friendships, ISBN 1-55945-138-6

Can Christians Have Fun?, ISBN 1-55945-134-3

Caring for God's Creation, ISBN 1-55945-121-1

Christmas: A Fresh Look, ISBN 1-55945-124-6

Competition, ISBN 1-55945-133-5

Dealing With Death, ISBN 1-55945-112-2

Dealing With Disappointment, ISBN 1-55945-139-4

Doing Your Best, ISBN 1-55945-142-4

Drugs & Drinking, ISBN 1-55945-118-1

Evil and the Occult, ISBN 1-55945-102-5

Genesis: The Beginnings, ISBN 1-55945-111-4

Guys & Girls: Understanding Each Other, ISBN 1-55945-110-6

Handling Conflict, ISBN 1-55945-125-4

Heaven & Hell, ISBN 1-55945-131-9

Is God Unfair?, ISBN 1-55945-108-4

Love or Infatuation?, ISBN 1-55945-128-9

Making Parents Proud, ISBN 1-55945-107-6

Making the Most of School, ISBN 1-55945-113-0

Materialism, ISBN 1-55945-130-0

The Miracle of Easter, ISBN 1-55945-143-2

Miracles!, ISBN 1-55945-117-3

Peace & War, ISBN 1-55945-123-8

Peer Pressure, ISBN 1-55945-103-3

Prayer, ISBN 1-55945-104-1

Reaching Out to a Hurting World, ISBN 1-55945-140-8

Sermon on the Mount, ISBN 1-55945-129-7

Suicide: The Silent Epidemic, ISBN 1-55945-145-9

Telling Your Friends About Christ, ISBN 1-55945-114-9

The Ten Commandments, ISBN 1-55945-127-0

Today's Faith Heroes: Madeline Manning Mims, Michael W. Smith, Mother Teresa, Bruce Olson, ISBN 1-55945-141-6

Today's Media: Choosing Wisely, ISBN 1-55945-144-0

Today's Music: Good or Bad?, ISBN 1-55945-101-7

What Is God's Purpose for Me?, ISBN 1-55945-132-7

What's a Christian?, ISBN 1-55945-105-X